AF481156

TOP 100

INTERESTING EARTH FACTS FOR KIDS

Animal Book for 6 Year Old
Children's Science Education Books

BABY PROFESSOR

Speedy Publishing LLC

40 E. Main St. #1156

Newark, DE 19711

www.speedypublishing.com

Copyright 2017

All Rights reserved. No part of this book may be reproduced or used in any way or form or by any means whether electronic or mechanical, this means that you cannot record or photocopy any material ideas or tips that are provided in this book

Earth, our home, is endlessly interesting. There is always more to learn and more to understand about this planet that we may think we already know pretty well. Jump into this book and learn 100 startling, silly, and amazing facts about the Earth and all of us who live on it.

OUR PLACE IN SPACE

1. Earth is the densest planet in the Solar System.

2. Over 100 million bits of junk from space ships and satellites are orbiting the Earth.

3. Earth travels through space at 67,000 miles an hour.

4. This is the only planet we didn't name after a Greek or Roman god.

5. Our Sun could hold one million Earths.

6. There are more than 7 quintillion grains of sand on the Earth. For every grain of sand, there are about 10,000 stars in the known universe.

7. Earth's powerful magnetic field protects from the effects of solar wind from the Sun.

8. It takes just over 8 minutes for light to travel from the Sun to the Earth.

9. Earth and the moon are the only places in our Solar System where there can be a solar eclipse.

10. If the Sun were the size of a beach ball, a golf ball would represent Jupiter and a pea would represent Earth.

11. For some reason, the area around Hudson's Bay in Canada has lower gravity than the rest of the world.

12. Without the Moon, Earth would rotate so rapidly that each day would last only six hours.

13. The rotation of the Earth is slowing down very gradually because of the way the Earth and the Moon interact. Scientists believe that, 900 million years ago, each Earth year had 481 18-hour days.

14. If we could use just 1/10,000 of the energy the Sun sends us each day, that would power everything we need to power.

15. The best place to find meteorites is Antarctica. It has no vegetation to hide them and no running rivers to carry them away. And, of course, you would have a lot fewer people competing with you to find meteorites!

ATMOSPHERE

1. Between one hundred and three hundred tons of cosmic dust enter the Earth's atmosphere every day.

2. Earth has over eight million lightning strikes every day.

3. The average lightning bolt is six miles long.

4. Our atmosphere is about 21% oxygen.

5. **The Amazon rainforest produces 20% of the world's oxygen.**

6. **Most rainbows are full circles. We don't see that most of the time because the Earth gets in the way of the bottom half.**

7. **As early as 1887, a house in Scotland had a system to provide the electricity it needed by wind power alone.**

8. **Clouds look puffy and float easily, but each one can contain millions of tons of water.**

WATER

1. Only about 3% of the Earth's water is fresh.

2. Of that 3%, two-thirds is locked up in ice.

3. The amount of ice in Antarctica equals all the water in the Atlantic Ocean.

4. More than 70% of our planet is covered in water.

5. Every cup of sea water you scoop up holds a tiny amount of gold.

6. Scientists have described over 300,000 species that live in the ocean, and they think that's only one third of the total.

7. Over 90% of all volcanic activity happens on the ocean floor.

8. The deepest part of the ocean, the Mariana Trench, is over 10 kilometers deep.

9. There is just ice at the North Pole, no solid land.

10. We have explored just 5% of the Earth's oceans.

11. The Atlantic is the saltiest of the oceans.

12. Only on the Earth, of all the planets and other bodies we know so far, can water exist as a solid, a liquid, and a gas.

13. The borders of oceans and seas are normally land. The Sargasso Sea, near Bermuda, is an area of calm water held with four ocean Atlantic Ocean currents as its boundaries. Seaweed and floating debris collect in the Sargasso Sea.

THE GROUND

1. The Earth is about 4.5 billion years old.

2. The crust of the Earth took a while to form. No rocks have been found yet that are older than four billion years.

3. The oldest fossils that we have found, of living organisms of any kind, are less than 3.9 billion years old. We have no record of the very first beginnings of life on the Earth.

4. The continents move away from, or toward, each other about two centimeters a year.

5. The world's largest earthquake was magnitude 9.5, in Chile in 1960.

6. "Earth" is from the Old English word "Eorthe", meaning "soil".

7. Between 10 and 20 volcanoes are erupting around the Earth every day.

8. The Sahara Desert covers about a third of Africa.

9. One third of Earth's dry land is partly or completely desert.

10. One teaspoon of soil holds more living organisms than the whole human population.

11. There are 500,000 earthquakes around the world each year.

12. People notice about 100,000 earthquakes a year.

13. About 100 earthquakes each year cause significant damage.

14. About 90% of earthquakes each year happen around the edges of the Pacific Ocean.

15. Yellowstone National Park in the United States is the top of an ancient super volcano. The last time it erupted, before humans had evolved, it threw a plume of ash all the way to Mexico.

16. Prairies are extensive grasslands, notably in western North America. They formed about 8,000 years ago and once covered almost half of what is now the United States.

17. Most of the rivers of the world start as small streams high up in mountains, and then follow the easiest course downward until they get to the sea.

18. The traditional way to estimate the height of a mountain was to climb it and then boil a pot of water and measure the water temperature. Water boils when the pressure of the steam trying to escape it is greater than the pressure of the air above the pot. At sea level, water boils at 100 degrees Celsius. At the top of Mount Blanc in the Alps, at 18,000 feet, water boils at 84 degrees Celsius. At the top of Mount Everest, at 29,000 feet, the pot would boil at 70 degrees Celsius.

19. Gangkhar Puensum, a mountain in Bhutan, is almost 25,000 feet high. It is the highest peak that nobody has managed to climb yet.

20. In deserts in over 30 different places around the world, there are sand dunes which "sing" (or chant, or buzz, or rumble) in the wind, like something between bees and a choir of men with deep voices. There are many theories for how and why this happens, but no one answer.

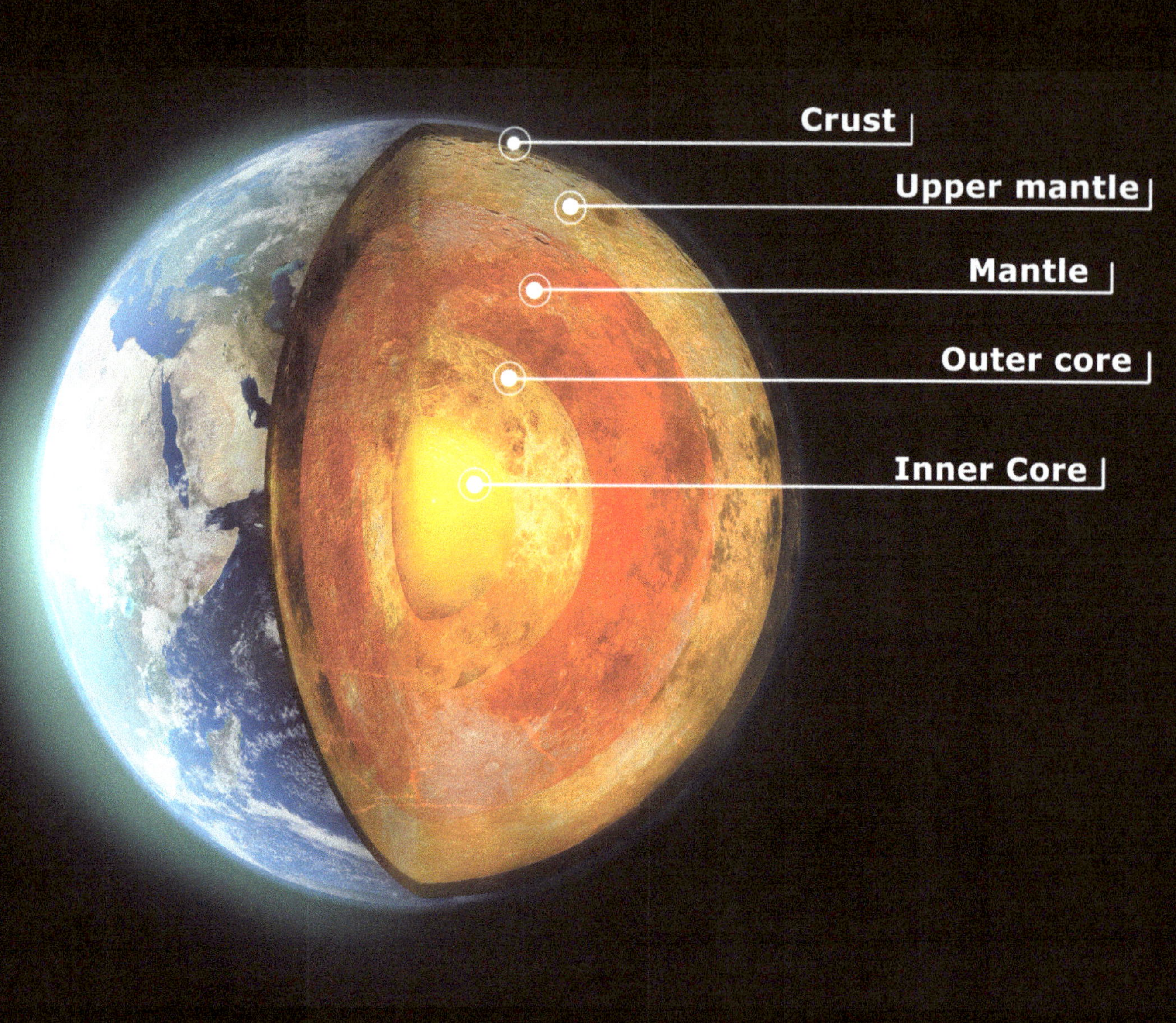

Crust
Upper mantle
Mantle
Outer core
Inner Core

UNDER THE GROUND

1. The temperature at the center of the earth, over 5500 degrees Celsius, is as hot as the surface of the Sun.

2. The Rio Hamza flows slowly through rock four kilometers below the Amazon River.

3. The Earth's core has enough gold that it could cover the whole surface of the Earth over a foot deep.

4. **People have explored 390 miles of Mammoth Cave in Kentucky. It may be more than 600 miles long.**

5. **Diamonds are more than three billion years old. They form under extreme heat and pressure about 100 miles inside the Earth, and then they get to the surface among the material a volcanic eruption brings up into the crust.**

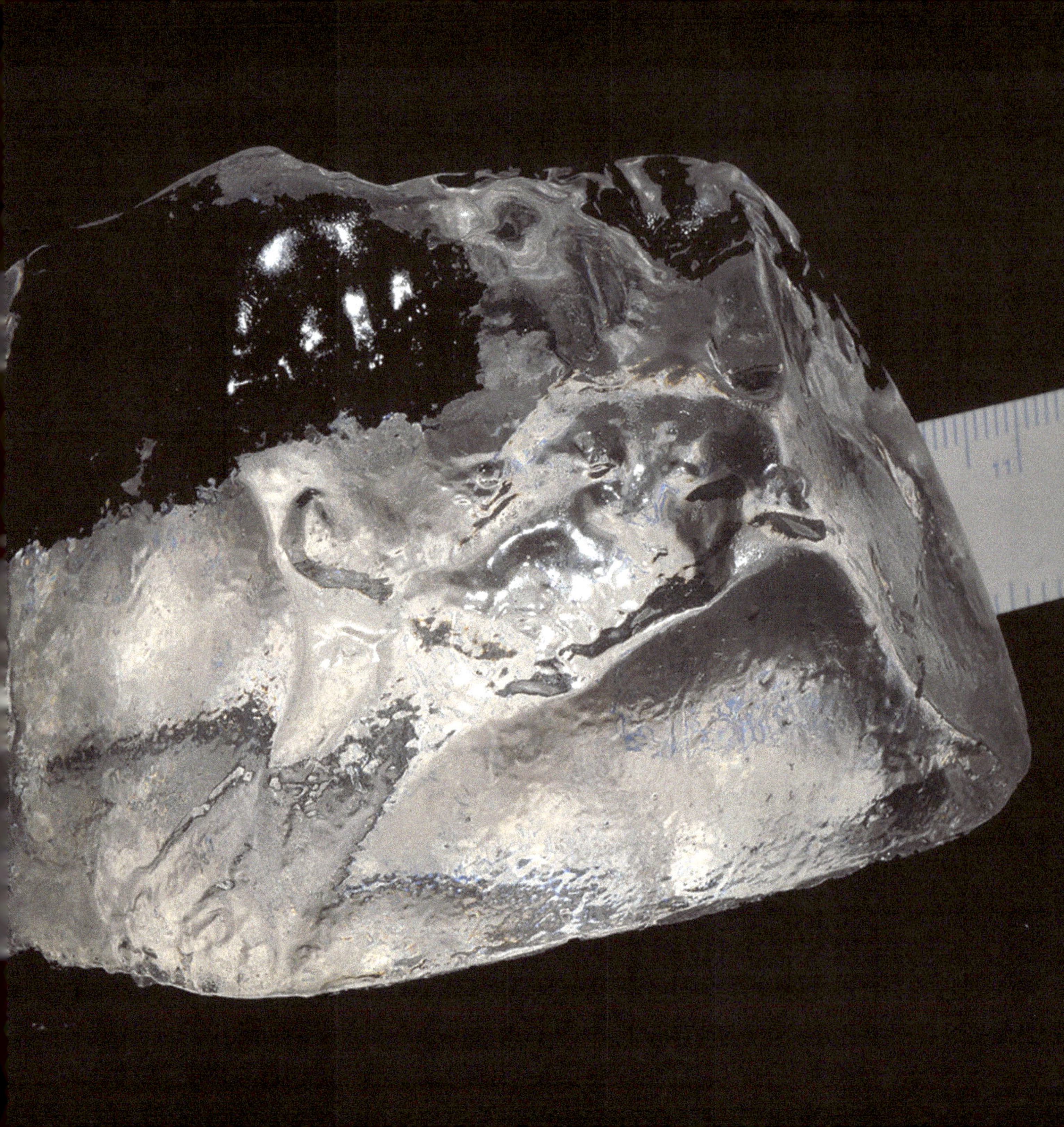

6. The extreme pressure inside the earth can take pure carbon and turn it into pure diamond.

7. The Cullinan Diamond, the largest one found so far, weighed almost a pound and a half. Jewellers cut it into nine large diamonds, some of which ended up among the British Crown Jewels in the Tower of London, and 100 smaller diamonds.

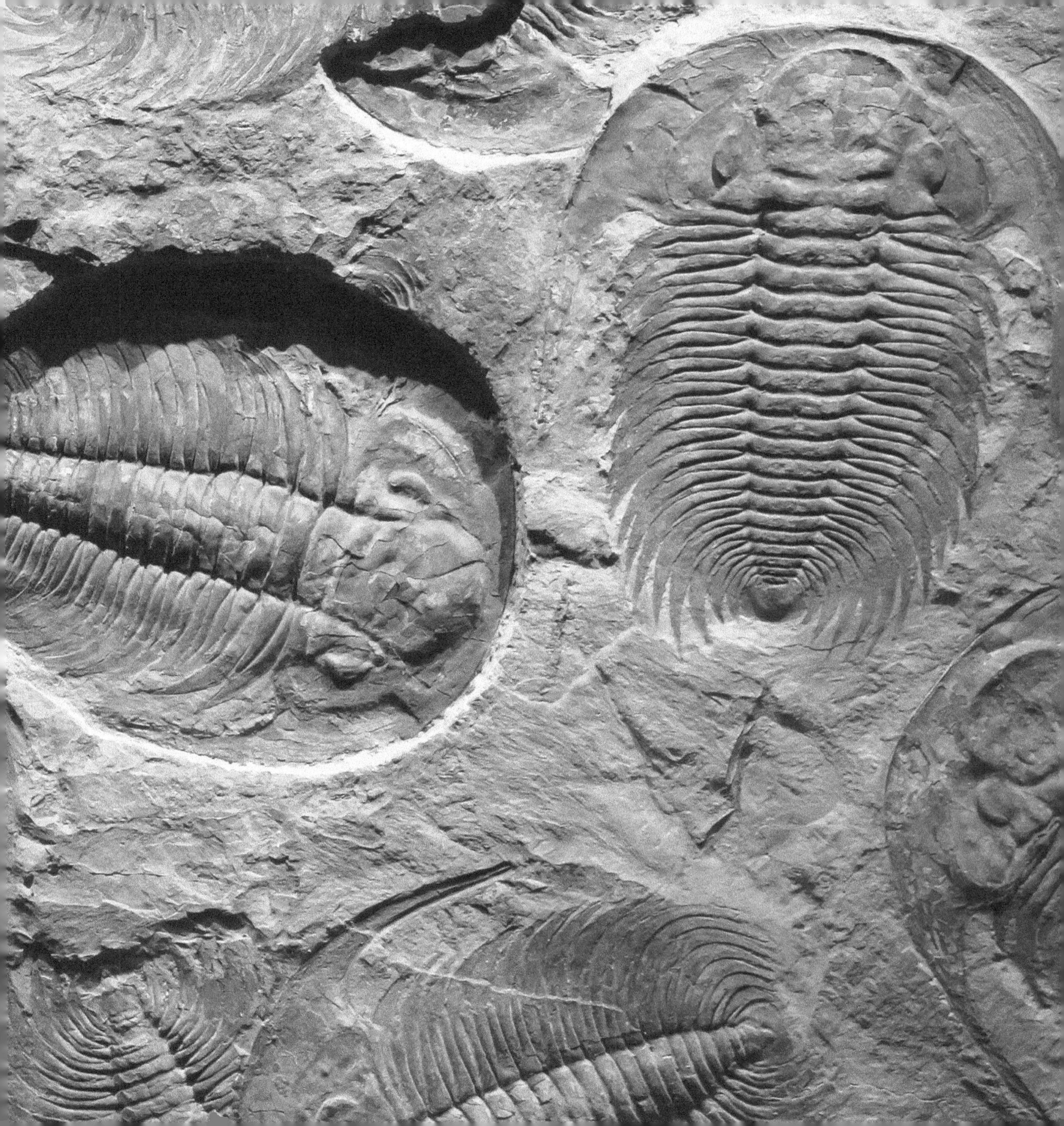

LIFE ON EARTH

1. Fossils of bacteria have been found that are 3.5 billion years old. That's before the atmosphere had oxygen.

2. Dry Valley, Antarctica, has not had rainfall in two million years.

3. We have only identified about 15% of the species on Earth.

4. When you are standing still, Earth carries you through space at a thousand miles an hour.

5. One third of land species live in the Amazon rainforest.

6. There are no black flowers on Earth.

7. Every part of the yew tree, except its berries, is poisonous to humans.

8. The tallest tree we have found, a redwood in California, is almost 400 feet tall.

9. Australia's Great Barrier Reef is the largest living structure on Earth.

10. Sharks kill about 10 people a year. People kill about 100,000 sharks a year.

11. There are ants on every land mass on Earth except for Antarctica and a few islands.

12. Fish have been swimming in the oceans for over 500 million years.

13. If you weigh 150 pounds at the equator, you would weigh 150.8 pounds at the North or South Poles. The effect of gravity is stronger at the poles.

14. In Texas, there's a town called "Earth". It's the only place on Earth, called "Earth".

15. About 25% of the medicines we use have their source in plants that grow in rainforests. Scientists have studied only about 1% of rainforest plant species so far.

16. The oldest non-clonal tree we have found is over five thousand years old. It lives in the Western United States. "Non-clonal" means it grew from a seed.

17. Quaking Aspen trees often live as a colony all sharing the same root system. The oldest such colony we have found is over 80,000 years old! As the original trees aged and died, new trees come up using the same root system.

18. A single bee would have to visit about 2 million flowers to make a pound of honey.

19. The elephant is the only animal species that can't jump.

EARTHLINGS

1. About 200,000 of us are born every day.

2. Every second, two people die.

3. There have been about 106 billion humans so far.

4. By 2050, our population could reach 9.2 billion.

5. If you map Earth's history to a 24 hour day, the dinosaurs died out at 11:40 pm and humans started at 11:54 pm.

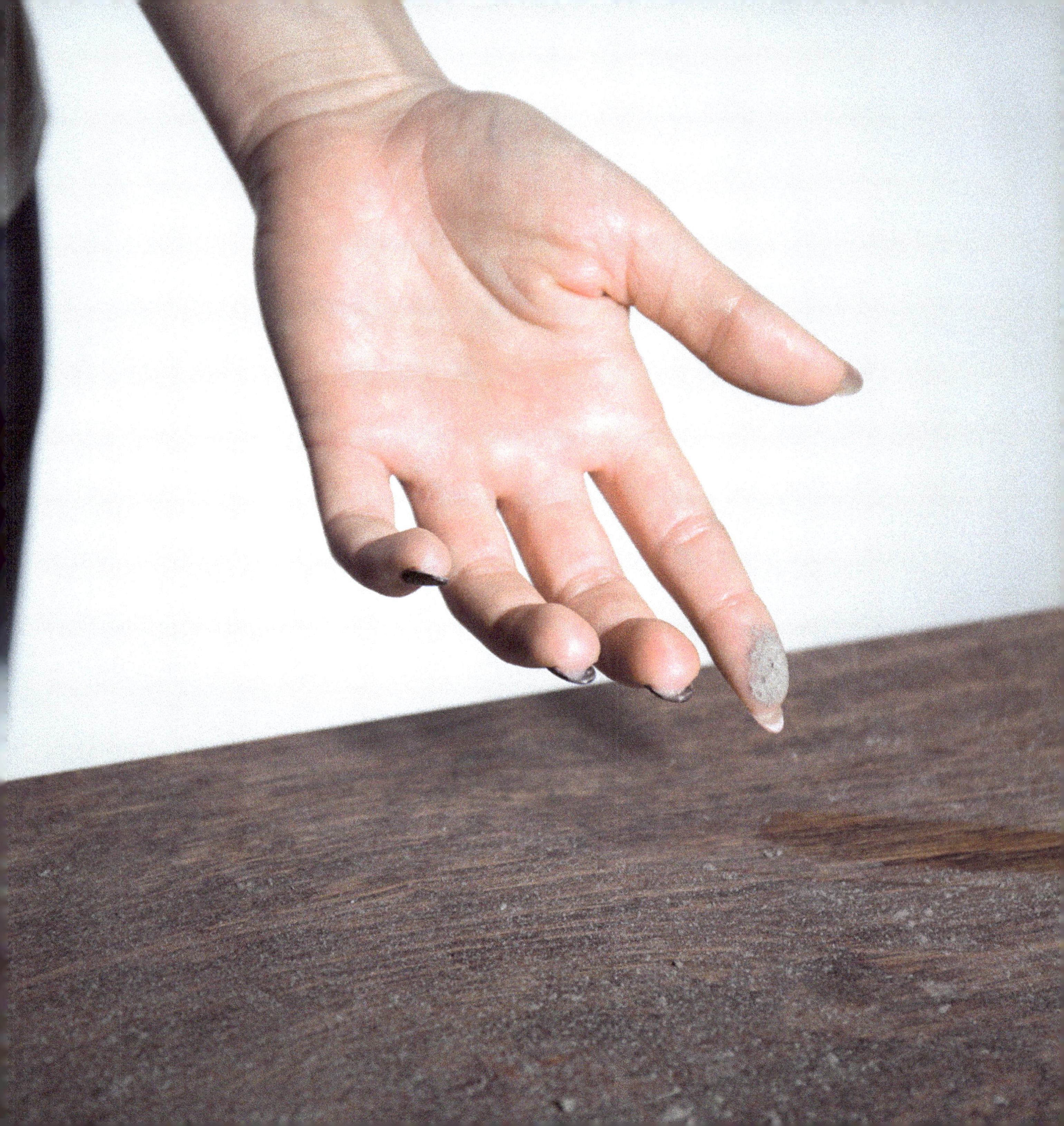

6. For every person, there are over 400 trees on Earth.

7. Six countries control 40% of the Earth's land area.

8. You shed about 600,000 tiny bits of skin every hour.

9. In your bedroom, the dust under your bed is mostly made up of dry, dead bits of your skin.

10. Your body has about 100,000 miles of blood vessels.

11. There's as much iron in your body as there is in a nail about three inches long.

12. Your sweat doesn't have a smell. What smells is when your sweat mixes with bacteria on your skin, in your shirt, or in your shoes.

13. All the bacteria in and on a grownup's body, added together, would weigh about four pounds.

14. Your tongue has a unique pattern, like your fingerprints. No two "tongue prints" are the same.

15. You blink so frequently that, even when you are awake, 10% of the time your eyes are closed.

16. You cannot snore and dream at the same time.

17. About 10% of people on earth are left-handed.

18. For every one of us humans on the Earth, there are 1.6 million ants.

EVEN MORE FACTS TO LEARN

Every one of these facts can lead to new questions, and lead you to find new answers. Read on in Baby Professor books about the Earth: it is your home, after all.

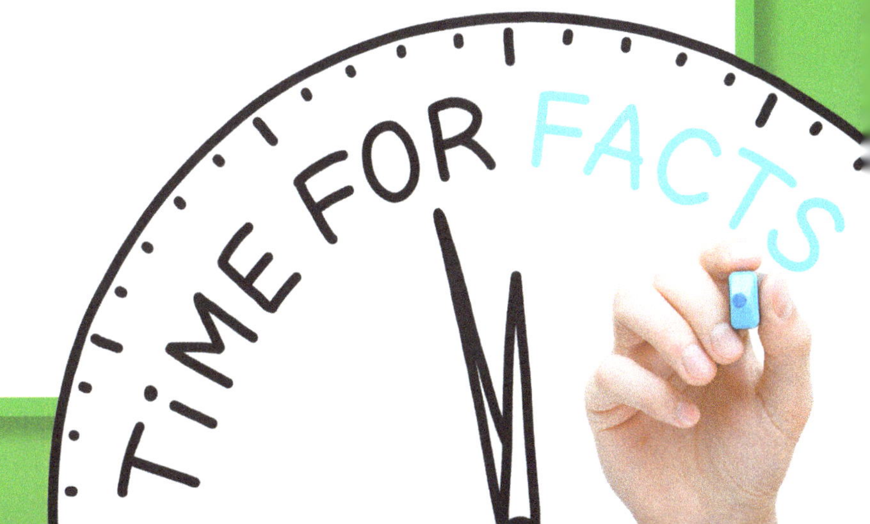

Visit
BABY PROFESSOR
EDUCATION KIDS
www.BabyProfessorBooks.com
to download Free Baby Professor eBooks
and view our catalog of new and exciting
Children's Books

www.ingramcontent.com/pod-product-compliance
Lightning Source LLC
Chambersburg PA
CBHW041729100726
47973CB00010B/153